Praising PRAISESONG

"in a city where nothing moves/A city with no mouths/to feed" we enter Ned Breslin's remarkable collection about feeding people on the Ukrainian frontline. These poems are carefully rendered with love and compassion for as people suffer in the deepest ways, they are also profoundly nourished. In this place of "unimaginable sorrow" we discover "Heavenly encounters/where God shines/in contradiction/in paradox."

~ Elizabeth Jacobson author of *There Are as Many Songs in the World as Branches of Coral.*

Born from direct service, this collection transforms witness into art, capturing the profound humanity that emerges amid the devastation of war. Ned Breslin doesn't merely observe Ukraine's resilience—he participates in it, serving food and warmth to civilians from Kherson to Kharkiv while bearing witness to their courage. *It is all too much.* These poems are like hugs *because hugs are needed.* They honor the Vitas and Sergiys, who, hearing explosions *(Hope survives faintly where gaps in the ruin exist),* choose to stay, who hold neighbors in their hearts and arms even as tanks gather under tarpaulin. Written with the intimacy of shared meals and the gravity of shared danger, this work reveals how poetry can become an act of faith and solidarity, documenting not just survival but the fierce tenderness that sustains communities under siege. A testament to both the power of presence and the necessity of bearing poetic witness.

~Iryna Starovoyt, author of *A Field of Foundlings*

In *Praisesong: Delivering Food on the Ukrainian Front Line,* Ned Breslin writes fourteen exquisite poems about the hope, care and resilience of people he has met living in war-torn Ukraine. We also learn about the courageous food fighters from World Central Kitchen. As a World Central Kitchen's Water, Sanitation and Hygiene Director, Ned Breslin has been on the front-line providing food and water to people in communities ripped apart by the destruction of war. His poetry captures the small but meaningful details of men and women trying to survive with dignity and an ethic of care despite being surrounded by betrayal, dead bodies, destroyed apartments and schools, and a lack of basic necessities. I was particularly moved by

"Thanksgiving in Kyiv," which captures the traumatic experience of a red-capped woman wearing a "gray winter jacket, clearly not her own." When given a gift of a cup of coffee, she "ever so slightly returns to herself." As the poem continues, we see her family, her bombed apartment, family photographs on the floor, and her young child, whom she picks up and holds. Every poem in this book helps us feel the devasting experience of Ukraine's war, but also the ways in which neighbors help each other with whatever resources they have. *Praisesong* is a powerful book of poetry.

~Beth Franklin, Executive Director of the Colorado Poets Center and emerita professor in English as a Second Language at the University of Northern Colorado

This past week, I spent time with our team visiting communities living along the front line, meeting people who, in the harshest conditions, continue to live on their own land, in their own homes, caring for their animals.

I simply cannot imagine the courage it takes, nor how deeply one must love one's home and Ukrainian identity, to risk one's life every day.

It was there that I truly understood: by providing food to these people, we are not just feeding them—we are showing them that they are not alone, and we are supporting their patriotism, which is an extraordinary source of strength for the Ukrainian people.

Praisesong tells our story. Our story of feeding, our story of caring for those caught on the frontline, our story of compassion and action that shows we will never abandon anyone.

~ Юлія Стефанюк (Yuliya Stefanyuk), Response Director for Ukraine, World Central Kitchen

Praisesong

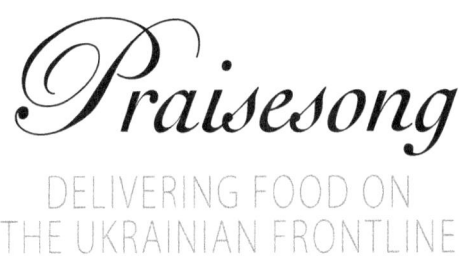

Praisesong

DELIVERING FOOD ON
THE UKRAINIAN FRONTLINE

NED BRESLIN

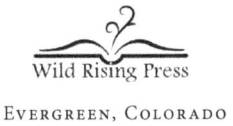

Wild Rising Press

EVERGREEN, COLORADO

Book Design: Mary M. Meade
Editor: Judyth Hill

First Edition
ISBN 978-1-957468-43-3

This book is dedicated to my loving family,
who are always Heaven to me

—LINDSEY, KIMBERLEY, JEMMA, AND LILLIAN

Earth's crammed with Heaven;

And every common bush afire with God;

But only he who sees, takes off his shoes

—ELIZABETH BARRETT BROWNING

NOTE TO READER

The Biblical references are all from the NRSV (New Revised Standard Edition).

All references to Thomas logia are from Lynn C Bauman, *In Trouble and In Wonder: A Spiritual Commentary on the Gospel of Thomas* (Longview Texas: Praxis Publishing, 2014).

I use the name Yeshua throughout—the English transliteration of Jesus's Hebrew name. I do this because there is something mystical, something like a warm blanket wrapped around me, when I hear his Hebrew name.

Contents

Forever Changed

Forever changed
it is here
I forever changed

Kateryna's truth floods
the too-still air
in a city where nothing moves

A city with no mouths
to feed

Where dogs and cats
who once roamed streets
are absent

Where no birds sing
nesting elsewhere

A silent city of fallen buildings
spilling into roads
denying passage

Kateryna's words
seek consolation
as sun dives for darkness

It was a technical college
and this, this wreckage lying before you
was a dormitory
for first-year students

Students who slept, ate, laughed, studied
to build our country

Pieces of furniture
once in service
wear the face of trash

Clothes designed
to comfort, bedazzle
have lost their warmth, their shine

Books written
to open minds to possibility
lie listless, torn, dismembered
sentences now incomplete

Wreckage monitored
by smirking mortar shells
celebrating the damage they caused

I needed to bring you here
because it is here
I realized
there would be no going back
to the world I knew and loved

Kateryna's husband Evgeny
nods, in chorus

Nods as a Holy wind
embraces Kateryna's words
to awaken a listless city
as Divine hand cradles and halts
the setting sun

Sun concentrates its powers
thrusting our shadows
infused with heart
deep into an entranceway

Deeper than we could go
alone

Our shadows linger in hallways
mingle with settled dust
listening, searching

Hover as footprints
where 18-year-olds
once wandered
and wondered
look up

Some footprints
full and flush on dusty floor
awaken, frozen in place

Others, frantic
shaking in terror
running in fear
searching for escape
emerge under shadows' gaze

Footprints that lie on sides
silenced in rubble
now call forth

Shadows whisper
We see you
as scale of loss is revealed

Our hearts miss a beat
tears well up and fall
bathing footprints now seen
as Yeshua taught [1]

Shadow tears caress
footprints now witnessed
as Mary modelled [2]

Tears infused with Divine care
mourn, honor
the footprints of 18-year-olds
who froze, fled, fell

Dust-covered floor
moist with tears
awash in remembrance
as Divine hand releases sun

Sun resumes its journey
bringing our shadows back close
our hearts shattered by the loss

Forever changing us
in a thin place
on the front line
of a war of unimaginable sorrow

---

[1] Mark 14:12–16; John 13:1–14:7
[2] John 12:1–8; Mark 14:3–9; Matthew 26:6–13 and a slightly different take on all
this in Luke 7:36–50

When Heaven and Earth Embrace

The place we call Heaven
is here [3]
so Yeshua says

Not up there
where birds sing and soar
not in the sea
where fish dive and frolic [4]
but rather here
on earth

Where we walk
play
celebrate
cause havoc

The Bible flows
with stories of encounter
meeting God in the actual, in the beauty
in the mess, in the mystery

Heavenly encounters
where God shines
in contradiction
in paradox

---

[3] Luke 17:21; Matthew 3:1–2; Matthew 4:17; Matthew 16:19 about the relationship
between Heaven and earth, which I find particularly powerful; Matthew 19:14;
see also the Gospel of Thomas, Logia 113 and 97
[4] Gospel of Thomas, Logion 3

Imploring us to create
a Heaven-filled world
when we have eyes to see

Cosmic eyes revealing Heaven
on earth, where we tread

Sadly
I do not see
with the eyes
that Yeshua beseeches us
to open

I am far too often absent
not present
in the moment
in the actual
where God waves

No ...
my eyes are blurred
by earthly bling

Riches, status
titles, validation
shame, guilt
all those things Yeshua gently suggests
distract us from the Divine

I thus desperately need
thin place encounters
to startle me awake

Thin places
where a veil glimmers
a threshold welcomes
and declares
Come in and build
with Me

Thin place occasions burst
in places of beauty and wonder
where Heaven entices

On mountains of such wow
our breath needs a moment
to catch up

In rivers of such grace
our body can't escape
the loving caress of flowing water

Along pathways
where famous feet have wandered
inspiring us to continue

Places of sheer beauty
bursting with the Divine
calling us home

And …

I find to my amazement
the Divine radiating
in places of profound horror

Because thin places erupt
where tears course our souls
pain and loss multiply
fear resides
death lurks and steals

Imploring us to accompany the Divine
as horror envelops

I encounter Heaven
presenting to face horror
in the garb of unselfish service

Places where
it would be easier
to turn and run away

Delivering, in this story ...
food

Food to nourish, witness, console

Food confirming to those left behind
you are not
forgotten

This is a tale of teams
delivering food
in a war

Inviting us to experience
Heaven on earth
amidst the rubble

I am thrust
away from the absence blinding me
into the present
when I am blessed to witness
thin places blossom
when others are cared for
as Yeshua modelled
mirroring God's love

When it would be easier
to claim God has abandoned us

Thin places sparkle
countering those trying to create
a Heaven-less world

Thin places glisten
to repulse those unleashing evil
trying to reshape the world in their image

Thin places shimmer
when darkness tries to envelop
compelling us instead to come forth

Thin places awaken us
to God's presence
amidst the horror, tears, pain

When eyes, newly opened in service
reject attempts to silence Heaven
with bombs, tanks, gunfire

Allowing us to marvel
as love combats terror

in embrace, in care
for those harmed

When Heaven penetrates the darkness
on the front lines
in a corner of this planet
we call Ukraine

Every Spark is Gathered

Residents encircle Vita
as tank guns wait
peeking from under tarpaulin

A blast followed by gunfire
causes some to awkwardly jump

Others look down
drop belongings as unsteady hands
move to protect exposed heads

Vita pauses to let neighbors
find their balance
in a small village outside of Kostyantynivka
in the highly contested Donetsk Oblast

A village with Russians to one side
Ukrainians on the other
waiting for orders to advance

Inhabited by weary Ukrainian civilians
living between two armies
in dispirited houses with open lesions
along gutted roads desperately clinging to frail bridges
barely connected to the rest of Ukraine

Filled with residents
seeking solace and comfort
circling a woman who remained
as she could not abandon her neighbors

A woman who would not leave
friends who cannot fathom
being internal refugees in their homeland

Standing with elders who cannot bear
the physical, the mental toll
such disruption would exact
in parts of Ukraine they do not know

Residents gather
for food and connection
as Vita takes in her neighbors
knowing tanks hiding under tarpaulin
will eventually emerge
will eventually roar
turning villages into battlefields

Vita holds each neighbor
in her heart
before eyes shift
past the gathered group

Searching for those
who have yet to arrive

Sergih and his team
start handing out food
but residents insist on a hug
first

Food and hugs are shared
as bullets and bombs ring out
while Vita stands back, mutters
Where are the missing lights?

A once-silent bird sings
guns fall silent
a warm silence descends
and Heaven sparkles
in the presence of a shard seeker

The giveaway is the word
light

Creation midrash [5]
speaks of a time before time
before the Birther of the Cosmos [6]
utters first words [7]

Divine, never-spoken words
first contained expectantly
in a cosmic vessel

Cosmic vessel bursts
into shards, into sparks
when first words are spoken

Shards, sparks scatter throughout the cosmos
finding a home in each person
in each rock and blade of grass
in each star

---

[5] Howard Schwartz, *Tree of Souls: The Mythology of Judaism* (Oxford: Oxford University Press, 2004), 122–124.

[6] Birther of the Cosmos is one of the powerful, mystical Aramaic-inspired counter interpretations of the "Our Father" start of the Lord's Prayer. See the blessed work of Neil Douglas-Klotz for more.

[7] Genesis 1:3

In each inhale
on every exhale
uniting us with the Divine

Shards within us all
dreaming of repair
in a cosmic kintsugi
bringing us safely home to the Divine

Vita invites this heavenly purpose
into our presence
as she is stirred by Divine light
in the hearts and souls of neighbors

Neighbors whose Divine spark
remains lit, despite the impending battle
meant to extinguish

Vita orchestrates
this unmistakable thin place encounter
noting who is present, who is absent
yet still aflame

Shard seeker begins
with a whisper
to an elderly woman in line
who nods, reaching out both hands

First to hug those sharing food
because hugs are needed
and then
with tear-filled eyes
tells us,

I am here for myself
and my neighbor Svetlana

Vita knows Svetlana
Vita asked me to collect food
for my family, for Svetlana's family

Svetlana's family is not here
they are there, in their home

You can ask Vita if you wish
she wants me to help
my neighbor Svetlana

An absent spark seen by Vita
because Svetlana's light
glows bright as God intends

Heaven pulsates as shard seeker
continues looking for light
beyond those in front of her

Vita now speaks
with an elderly man
whose empty cart on wobbly wheels
waits expectantly

He speaks as his cart is filled with food
I thought I would come today and help
even though I am so scared

I am slow and my cart
does not walk well
anymore

I could not take a single step
outside my house
with all the terrifying noise
the last time you came

But Vita made sure
I received my food

She has now asked me
to add one more food bag to my cart

To deliver this other food bag
to the widow who peers out her broken window
afraid like me

Old man blossoms in service to a widow
as Vita effortlessly links
present light with absent light
the absent light of neighbors
who are not forgotten

Because shard-seeker Vita
is incapable of missing any light that shines
through the cosmos

Any light that is
alight, even in a war [8]

A mom with blank-eyed children
eyes with gathering tears
approaches on this front line
reaches for food, whispers

---

[8] *Light shines from the center of a being of light and illuminates the whole cosmos*—Gospel of Thomas, Logion 24

Vita lives near me
Vita cares for me and my children
Vita always watches for us
never forgets, never forgets us

As shard seekers
are known to do

This dance continues
some reach for one bag, others for two
with Divine light flaring
through clothes and tears and absence
harnessed by a shard seeker

Thin place outstaring tanks, artillery, soldiers
whispering
I Am here, with you

Crowd dwindles, and new friends,
now, with food,
make their way back home

Walking under caring gaze
of shard seeker who now reaches
for her food bag
and one other

She offers thanks
hoping we will return
and moves on
with an extra food bag for a light
nobody could help on this day

A light Vita still sees
as Yeshua teaches us
because all lights
even the one that is lost
must be found and held [9]

She ignores tanks
and finds unity with the Divine instead
food bags offering balance
across a village between two armies
gathering every spark

---

[9] Luke 15:1–7; Matthew 18:10–14; Gospel of Thomas, Logion 107

It Is All Too Much

A missile strike on an apartment
forever lacerates eyes, heart, soul

We are confronted by overwhelm
when standing before the post-strike wreckage
in places people once called home

Knees buckle
imagining the terror in plummet
as floor unravels, falls
until the ground gives no more

Concrete and rebar
table leg
what looks like a sofa
but could be part of a bed
doll parts unwelcomely married to Legos
shoes without feet

All unable to escape

Between and within
the smoldering debris caused by missile
are people

Children separated from parents
now lost in catastrophe
covered in ash
suffocating in darkness

Hope survives faintly
where gaps in the ruin exist

Gaps holding space, enough air
for a person shattered by it all
to hold on, until aid comes

Alive for now
caught between brick, painting, chair, photo of mom

Each breath cautiously taken
as any adjustment could empower gravity
to allow rubble to fill gaps

Do
not
move

Inhale
exhale
but do not move

Hold on
until found, pulled forth
birthed anew
from rubble

The apartment complex
in the city of Zaporizhzhia
stood no chance as Russian missile intruded
on a cold morning in March

Air raid sirens
sounded day after day
night after infuriating night
becoming part of the rhythm
of the city

Rhythm without melody

Sirens in January
sirens in February
sirens in March

Sirens so regular
many decide to ignore these alerts
screaming *incoming*

Ignore and stay in home, in bed
desperate to sleep
fighting to maintain some normalcy
in the madness

Who can blame residents
wrapped in blankets, in bed at 2 AM
who roll over, in winter, in dark, in exhaustion

The 2 AM darkness strangles light
masking the magnitude
of the horror

Sun slowly illuminates
to the extent we can absorb
the totality of the loss

Rescue teams call out
ears tuned for human sound

Neighbors frenetically scan
wondering if a loved one's apartment
stands or has fallen

Borscht, coffee, sandwiches and comfort
flow for those who rescue, who witness
who will inevitably shed tears

Screams of *no*
ring out

Tears blend with soil
snow, ice, debris

Few can stand
as stretchers collect neighbors
telling a story by their movement

Some stretchers move slowly
silently carrying a loved one
who has left us

Other stretchers are carried in a rush
scrambling across unsteady ground
as paths are cleared to allow a loved one
pulled from wreckage
still with breath
to pass

In this swirl
of pain and movement and tears
a woman gently repositions me
to face her

Uneven ground
mixed with horror
keep her off balance

Grey hair
coat buttoned tightly
gloveless red hands scream cold

Hands exposed for too long
because she came fast, rushing here

She wants to speak
but the silent exhale of cold breath
is all that escapes

She looks at me
at the building
as Alex joins
curious and ready to help
as words will surely arrive

With eyes full of tears yet to fall
she finally speaks

I heard the explosion

I live close by, and I was worried
my best friend lives
in this building

She is older than me
she can't get out of bed anymore

I spend my days with her
feeding her
laughing, reading, remembering
because she is my best friend

The explosion shook me awake
and I worried
was it in her neighborhood?
maybe her apartment?
I could not be sure

So I texted her

I waited for a response
but I am ... so tired

I fell back asleep

I fell ...
back asleep

When I woke up
there was no response to my text

I came here, anxious
because I fell asleep
after I sent the text

I immediately knew
she was gone
her apartment was there

Red gloveless finger
points towards collapsed building
while eyes stay fixed on me

She loses her way
and falls unsteadily into my arms
head colliding, resting on shoulder

Tears finally release
spilling pain, sorrow, moisture
freely onto my jacket

My tears follow
finding her coat
as Heaven opens in this flood of emotion
no longer contained

Tears reveal
a threshold that mirrors the tears
Yeshua shed for his dear friend Lazarus

Surely a thin place pulsed
as Yeshua approached a grave
in tears
as people looked on
before the miracle, all those years ago

Yeshua opened a thin place
then and now
because Heaven too sheds tears [10]

Eyes assimilate in thin place embrace
as Heaven unfolds

Trees surrounding wreckage
come into focus over her wet shoulder

Trees …
full of clothing

---

[10] John 11:35

Clothing that leapt out, escaping
as the violent blast thrust people
and their belongings
downward

Shirts, coats, pants
a red sweater

Seen clearly now
through falling tears
engulfed in sobs
echoing through a Heaven
in mourning

Clothes watch as stretcher emerges
from the rubble

Slow-moving stretcher
met by a holy mournful breeze

Spirit fills arms of red sweater
extending, reaching for the stretcher

Arms extend in sorrow
in pain
in … gratitude

Sweater waves for a loved one
on a slow-walking stretcher

Bathed in tears
from above, from below
as woman whose tears seek solace in my embrace
gently pulls back

Tears lovingly cradle her face
bless my shoulder
as sweater arms wave
and a new voice
of profound truth
arises

You must tell them …
I am Russian
I have lived here
my whole life

I am Russian
and this is too much

They have stolen my best friend
For what?
For what!

No more
No more!

You tell them, tell them
this is too much

Words which Alex
Russian by birth
courageously, graciously
translates between sobs

She nods ever so slightly
steps slowly away, waves

Her red hands mimic sweater
blend with tears

falling across this site
across Ukraine
across this thin place

Joined with cosmic tears
flowing with abandon
because this is too much
even for Heaven

Welcomed In

I met Mykola
in a mysteriously, marvelous way

Exiting a feeding site
holding a sealed box with logo

From a humanitarian agency
who knew this community outside of Kherson
hungered

I wonder aloud whether he knows
what food awaits
inside sealed box

He smiles
as skin around eyes crease

They are all the same
the food is always the same

The only difference are the logos
that safely guards the food
inside

The logo tells me who cares
tells me who is kind

His smile deepens
as he places box with logo on the car
between us, as if to share

And without pause
he lists what he imagines is inside
telling us who cares, who is kind

Smile deepens when finished
creases around eyes extend beyond
as he opens box

A box full of food
he named correctly
when contents were hidden

He laughs from places deep within
and exclaims

You must come with me
to meet my wife Olena
you must come with me
now

Moving forward with a slight limp
he begins to clean out his car

Tools asleep on front seat
now snuggle in back
placed by Mykola
with reckless abandon, simmering joy
as if tools should be resting there already

He removes a deactivated landmine
a landmine made impotent
and spent cartridges
to make space for a stranger

And when space has been made
seat and floor welcoming
he steps back, inviting me inside

I could not go, not on this day
but a promise is made
to return to meet Olena
a promise to come inside their home
next time

Mykola shrugs
as the creases surrounding eyes
lose their way

Resigned, he simply asks
for a photo to remember

Mykola pulls close, holds my hand
as photo captures all

Box of food full of kindness
peeks out rear window
recording promises made

Now thin places glisten
oh, they astonish
when promises are kept
because Heaven rejoices
when relationships are watered

We return to greet Mykola and Olena
who embrace strangers like family

Smiles with creases on their two faces
search for the creases on our faces
as hands beckon, welcoming us inside

Heaven's joy shifts
into a heavenly hum
tuned to our footsteps crossing thresholds
from gate to doorway to hallway
calling us deeper inside

A hallway whose walls are covered in photos
honoring memory, memorializing family
cheering in sync with heavenly hum

A kitchen awaits
with set table, chairs inviting
bread, wine, a bottle of vodka
patiently calling as borscht bubbles on stove
and fills the air with flavor

We brought food to share
but our contribution
was laid aside, without malice

Dismissed by Olena
who cooked all day
inside her thin place kitchen

We sit together around the table
bread with borscht pass lips to belly
a journey that bread, blessed by borscht
must travel

We share food
share stories, laughter

until Mykola raises a glass, pauses
in this thin place
as Heaven clothes him
in song and courage

A tear emerges
against the flow of the meal
and falls

A tear
pouring from heart

I was so scared
so scared as bombs dropped
and bullets flew
there ...

He looks beyond walls and window
staring outside, speaking from inside
as tears course down his cheeks

I stayed inside this house for 3 months
I would not leave
because I was so afraid

I looked out windows
I gazed at sky
I kept Olena in sight
I tried to look strong
but I shook with fear

As bombs dropped and bullets flew
shaking while trying to be strong

Tear follows tear
until an unfamiliar tear falls
different from those who ventured out first

Tears of shame make way
for tears of gratitude

Kateryna came
brought food in bags with logo
showing she cares
showing she is kind

She did not make me go outside
to collect the food
but brought the food inside
so that I did not have to go
outside

Mykola settles, tears slow
and no further words follow
or are needed

A great truth shared with strangers
treated like family

Olena's hand presses into the silence
offering a small dollop of borscht
gently placed in Mykola's bowl
now seasoned with tears

We pause, bearing witness
as glasses are emptied
bowls filled anew
bread basks in soup yet again
and passes lips to belly

Time passes without notice
as happens in thin places

Door to kitchen swings open
and Kateryna enters with more strangers
who will be treated as family

Room is fuller, richer
as space is made at a table
where room can always be made

And it is here
when Mykola stands
tears building for a second time
as words once again escape

Our house
Olena and my house
is the only house
that bombs and bullets missed

Kateryna nods in knowing way
her light comforting Mykola's tears

Neighbors think Olena and I
are spies … Russian spies

Russian spies who live in a house
standing alone
missed by bullets and bombs
protected from harm

Russians in a house
intentionally missed
by bullets and bombs

Sobs expand beyond limit
as a further truth is spoken

You came
when I was accused of betraying my country
the country I love

You Kateryna
came ...

And Yeshua's words from so long ago
find expression in the words
Kateryna offers

I know who you are
and I know
what you are not

I know you and Olena have suffered
you and Olena have been
falsely accused

Yet I am nourished
nourished to know you
to know you and Olena

A Heavenly purr fills room
hearts dancing with each beat
as we gather, are blessed

in the company of those
falsely persecuted [11]

A Heaven on earth where people
are truly seen, despite the lies
that gain ground when falsely judged

Heaven is fueled
by sobs watering truth
sobs setting us free
as Heaven beckons us
inside

---

[11] Matthew 5:10–12. An Aramaic interpretation of this beatitude offered by
Neil Douglas-Klotz resonates even more forcefully—"Turning themselves to
ripeness are those being pushed beyond safe boundaries for the sake of honesty
and justice. They are renewed in the vision and power of the larger life vibrating
around them." Words that apply to Mykola, Olena, and Kateryna. Neil Douglas-
Klotz, *Revelations of the Aramaic Jesus: The Hidden Teachings on Life & Death*
(Virginia USA: Hampton Roads Publishing, 2022), 63.

Generosity Overflows

The city of Kherson kisses the Dnieper River
and has experienced
some of the fiercest fighting
in this unspeakable war

Many agencies rushed in
in early November 2022
when Russian forces retreated
to the sound of liberated survivors
singing of victory

People emerged with trauma-filled eyes
from the rubble of their homes
and scars of their experiences
as food finally flowed
through the post-battle wreckage
of this soiled, beautiful city

Survivors speak of generosity
reimagining how to share shelter, food, water
so all could taste despite bellies
screaming for more
all could sleep with some semblance
of roof overhead

We are rightly horrified
by the scarcity that unfolds
in famine and war

We simultaneously can marvel
at how generosity unfolds
in shocking scarcity

Generosity mirroring
what Yeshua taught, constantly [12]

Generosity challenging hoarding
refusing to let the fear and paucity
of food, water, shelter
lead to expressions of
only me

Kherson rightly became the focus
of much-needed attention
by humanitarian agencies

Lots of people in a once densely packed city
whose access to food and water
was and remains tenuous
as Russia seeks recapture

In the rush to support Kherson
other smaller villages
that withstood battles and evil
could easily be bypassed

These villages are harder to see
scattered across battlefields beyond city limits
where generosity also blossomed
when evil intruded

Join me in one such village
where fighting had been fierce
and generosity flourished, largely out of sight

---

[12] Cynthia Bourgeault invites us to raise our eyesight beyond individual Bible
verses to the overall flow of the Yeshua's life, which was founded on many things,
including generosity and abundance. See for instance Cynthia Bourgeault, *The
Meaning of Mary Magdalene: Discovering the Woman at the Heart of Christianity*
(Boulder: Shambala Publications Inc, 2010), 104–105.

Ukrainian soldiers originally defended this small village
by taking up positions in Ukrainian homes
homes stretching down one street
and up another

Homes that at one time
hosted parties filled with laughter
homes where tears could release
homes drenched in boredom
homes that at one time were safe

Homes that became unsafe as war waged
now sheltering Ukrainian soldiers
who hid behind walls
firing back as Russian aggressors sought control

The population was always small
under 200 souls at its most robust

Many left, a few stayed
hiding on the ground
in rubble behind walls
in basements not fully caved in

Remained in their village
once filled with laughter, tears, boredom
because this is home

Russia captured this small village
homes who once housed Ukrainian soldiers
now housed soldiers wearing Russian insignia

Residents who remained
provided much needed intel

allowing Ukrainian soldiers
to reposition, to rethink

Intel delivered as Russian soldiers
shot, drank, slept, hurled insults, threatened
and ultimately lost themselves

Lost themselves in the homes they had invaded
dwellings where invading soldiers
could not heal when oppressing

Critical intel in a key battle
that Ukraine's army won
forcing Russian soldiers into retreat

A small village liberated
to the sound of song
in the raising of a Ukrainian flag

A sound like those heard by Russian soldiers
who retreated from Kherson

The Ukrainian army, having won
surveyed the wreckage and moved on
from a supposedly insignificant village
easily forgotten as it barely existed

Julia and her team of food fighters
make sure food and water flows
in the city of Kherson
while never shifting eyes
from small villages that matter too

Yeshua always centered those unseen
those pushed aside, looked past
as happens too often

Yeshua centered those near pools
seeking healing, in parts of town
where people feared to tread [13]

Centering women at wells
who arrive late with fertile hearts open
despite being from a foreign tribe [14]

Centered those, like Yeshua himself,
who crossed borders into foreign lands
illegally, despite the risk of crossing [15]

Centered others
mirrored by Julia

Julia saw Oleg
whose intel changed the direction
of the fight for this village

She saw Oleg and one other family
a total of six people
who stayed

Oleg's home could no longer offer shelter
much like their neighbor
whose home no longer stood

---

[13] John 5:1–13
[14] John 4:4–30
[15] Mark 3:8

They stayed
finding ways to sleep
in cover

Found ways to collect water
even as pump damage
stopped water flow

Shrapnel jutting from what was once a kitchen
a kitchen who found a way to cook
scarce food to be shared

Bread divided and shared
as Yeshua did
all the time [16]

Neighbors who stayed, shared
generously

We were met by Oleg, with eyes full of heart
in this mostly forgotten village
after Russians fled and all rushed to Kherson

We offer a food kit and water
in the charred remains of a village marred in wreckage
with fields tainted by land mines

Oleg gently, politely
refuses our offering
of ingredients not seen in these parts
for some time

---

[16] Luke 5:27–32; Luke 7:36–50; Luke 10:38–42; Luke 24:28–32 are just a few
examples

Place it there please
there ...
please

I am grateful but I want to share
something with you
first ...

Oleg's eyes shine
as he leads us past
a part of his now caved-in home

Unclear what part of the home
this exactly is

Oleg is in no mood to provide an inventory
of damage caused

Without words he takes us into a sacred place
he wants to share before considering
our offering

Takes us to a row of wooden beehives
alive in grandeur
swarming with bees
who survived the madness

Bees departing hives
in search of nourishment
for self, for others

Bees napping in flowers
securing nectar, spreading pollen
returning to beehive where their haul is celebrated

Bees have always kept our world pulsing
in cosmic rhythm

Giving and building
sharing and offering
sweetness
when all seems so stale

Heaven announces itself
to the sound of bees in cosmic alignment
a sound tickling ears, igniting hearts
to the presence of Heaven
in the rubble

A gentle hand extends in the symphony
one welcoming hand on my shoulder
the other hand cradling
a jar of honey

Oleg is alight
with his gleaming gaze
and an infinite smile

Precious honey in giving hands
a jar overflowing in sweetness
produced by bees, harvested in a war
offered by a man who remained

A man who saw the world he lived in
with abundance to be shared generously
to remain sacred

I am someone who gives
who shares what I have

as we all have gifts
we all have gifts to share

None of us
none of us just receives

Words from beyond places
unlocking a thin place
pulsing through a written-off village

Oleg's generosity found resonance with cosmic breath
infused with Divine wisdom
dancing to a cosmic harmony
dripping with honey
mirroring Yeshua's words and actions

An unmistakable thin place
gushing with generosity, infused with care
transcending a world screaming
this is mine

This generous Heaven on earth
where we care for others

Found in unlikely places
amidst famine
in war, floods, hurricanes

Where a dollop of honey
infused with the generosity of bees
in the hands of neighbors who cannot imagine
a Heaven-infused world unable to share

Thin places posing the question
of why such generosity
seems so unusual

Thin places flowing with abundance
in unacceptable scarcity
at the center of catastrophes
inviting us to a reimagined world
with new definitions of bounty

Where we know of no alternative
but to share our bread, wine, clothes, presence
just to be sure [17]

Given from heart places
accommodating the pulse of the cosmos [18]

---

[17] Matthew 5:38–48

[18] From Sufi poet Mahmoud Shabestari's breathtaking poem "The Secret Rose Garden" calling out from Neil Douglas-Klotz, *Desert Wisdom: A Nomad's Guide to Life's Big Questions from the Heart of the Native Middle East* (Worthington OH: Arc Books 2011), 121.

Neighbors Reciprocate

Inga pauses each day
to honor the school
barely standing in front of her

As sun peeks through destroyed ceilings
and broken windows

Sunbeams glancing off branches
of the few trees still standing in the schoolyard
where she was once known
as headmistress

She has shepherded children
from first steps through graduation
for decades

She has cheered, cried, been lost, offered comfort
as headmistresses do

She wonders whether her beloved school
will ever breathe again

When war broke out
children and parents looked to her
as they always have

The weight of expectation
was altered in this new world
as school lay in pieces and expectations grew

I know all
all the children, all the adults

as many of my children
have now become adults

I knew in this time of war
that I must serve
serve differently

I knew I must weave
a special Ukrainian rug [19]
a rug of neighbors woven together
to care for one another

As food is delivered
Inga moves hands and fingers
as if weaving

Showing how every family
in her community is united
with a neighbor

Families woven together
to ensure all her former students
are blessed with presence and witness
by another

The weaving is intricate

Sometimes woven neighbors
live next door to each other

Other strands unite households
well known to each other
harnessed in strength

_____

[19] Ukrainian rugs are beautiful and special, so these words carry significant weight.

Sometimes this master weaver
braids strangers together
knowing their collective textures
will dazzle

And other times still
families are reunited because of deep friendships
forged and sustained
when as children they walked the halls
of her school

She admits there are times
when her newly woven rug
strains

Yet it holds and can be repaired
to stay strong, to comfort
in the madness

An explosion sounds
close enough to startle, far enough away
to allow people to gather cautiously
collecting food, wearily

Collecting food in Inga's driveway
in the shadow of a broken school
where all were welcome before the madness

And as the explosive sound of evil retreats
Inga reveals another purpose

It is not safe for all to gather
in my driveway
collecting food

If all came
if all stood here to collect food
and mourn the loss of our school, our lives, our safety
we would be seen more easily
and bombs would be sent

People come
they come and they are seen
they come and they collect
food for their family
and food for their neighbor

I listen when they come
to hear how each of my students
some who are now adults
are doing
as bombs are sent

If someone leaves
or if a bomb
steals a family and rips our rug
then we must reweave the network
reweave the rug

Reconnect a neighbor with another family
so nobody is without a neighbor

So nobody is unsupported
nobody is alone

Inga pauses as she recalls
the many times her rug
needed mending from such loss

When her rug needed to be patched
as war took former students away

The silence is broken
by the explosive sound of bombs striking

Inga returns from the pause
angry at the noise
offering a gift

Jesus told us to love our neighbor
to honor our neighbor
to stand with our neighbor
in the love you hold for yourself
for God [20]

Ever-present Heaven radiates awe
as Inga's words penetrate

Inga's tapestry of neighbors
guided by Yeshua's words
in step with Yeshua's actions
moisturizes Heaven's constant unfurling
as bombs are being sent

Allowing Heaven to hold ground
and refortify in a war
in front of the school
where she shepherded all

But who
who is your neighbor Inga?

---

[20] Matthew 22:37–40; Luke 10:27; Matthew 19:19; Mark 12:31; with seeds planted in Leviticus 19:18 and Deuteronomy 10:19

Another pause as tears in Inga's eye
gather, plummet
with a force drowning out explosions

I lost my husband
almost six months ago

He died in this house
because we could not get him to a hospital
as the war raged and destroyed my school

He died and I
I am now alone
with my daughter

We did not have a neighbor
like the others

I worried people might think
my neighbor would be favored

We stayed, organized
we wove our Ukrainian rug
my daughter and I
we did so ... alone

Heaven cradles Inga
as tear follows tear
as words with weight sink deep

It was so hard making sure
everyone had a neighbor

So hard making sure all who walked
in my school were cared for
by another

The pressure I felt
doing Jesus's work
in a home where my husband
no longer welcomes me
was too much

I fell ill
so ill

I could not breathe
as bombs were sent

I could not stand
as the responsibility for all this
grew

I collapsed in my house
and did not
stir

I woke up
woke up one day in a hospital
far away from my home
from my school

I looked up from bed in a hospital
and saw ... a teacher

One of my teachers at the foot of my bed
smiling

My daughter, she said,
is safe with a neighbor

We have kept your work going

we are all fed
we are all seen

Nobody is without a neighbor
nobody is alone

Inga pauses
Heaven radiates
and a smile finds space

The warm smile we have all felt
exploding across our face when we know
we are cared for

When we know we are not just
caring for others

Yes
I now have neighbors
all are my neighbors
all those who walked in my school
are my neighbors

And as Heaven radiates more vigorously
than explosions can rescind
Inga's smile deepens further
a tenderness for herself
is unmasked

And the world that Yeshua savors
with love for self and neighbor
with love from the Divine
unfurls in beauty in front of a school
teaching us all

Dogs Come Running

Dogs wait patiently
some distance away

Dogs waiting in Izium
just beyond a feeding site
sometimes in groups
sometimes alone

Izium is shrouded in cold
residents enveloped in weariness
after months under siege

Weary too
from looking over their shoulders
as fear weighs heavily in a city
once again under Ukrainian control

Russian soldiers still hover nearby
and spies are seen, rightly or wrongly
everywhere

Looking over shoulders in fear and uncertainty
exhausts

Food is scarce
electricity even more so
as transmission lines
to light and heat and refrigerate
vanished long ago

Buildings are weary
scarred and wounded

covered in soot stains
where missiles and mortars penetrated

Food fighters too
are weary

The weight of expectation
of witness
of sharing
of hugs blessed with kindness
nourishes and exhausts

War has left Izium residents
uncertain and weary
sinking in fear
as dogs
circle and wait
some distance away

The front line has shifted
just out of sight
yet still within reach

Izium is both cold
and hot

Bombs still scream as day bleeds into dusk
and residents gather for food
linger for comfort
shake in fear

Dogs mimic the elders of Izium
shrinking and ducking for cover
shaking noticeably

as booms ring out
magnified in ears, as happens to dogs

Feeding in Izium lasts all day
from first light
to when sun dives for sleep

Hot meals
tasting of home
coupled with food kits
honor today and bridge the gap
from today to a future visit

Food served against the backdrop
of destroyed stores
who will not return anytime soon

Meal sites change
as the sun dances across the sky
before diving to sleep

Pack up one site
when all are fed
move to the next site, across this vast city

Shifting feeding-site positions
to a chorus of boom and blast
so food and comfort can be delivered
as close as possible
to where people shelter

Distances reduced between shelter and food
so that elderly residents would not expose themselves

for too long
as bombs screamed

People gather at each new stop
in another part of the city
as dogs wait patiently

A woman walks forward
pauses as eyes search
for connection

She hesitates
to take the food being offered
and instead signals a yearning
for something to warm differently than food

Arms tentatively extend forth
as eyes meet
the eyes of another
in hope of reciprocity

A knowing smile
whispers *please*
when smiles are hard to rebuild
after the violence

Food fighters welcome
this invitation with open arms
and embrace

A woman and a food fighter
nestle in a hug
offering deep warmth on an unsafe front line

This marriage of food and embrace
travels and repeats
from site to site

As dusk expands
dogs noticeably come
a bit closer

Tails wave gently
calling out in silence
devoid of anger
seemingly wondering if the focus
would eventually turn to them

Dogs hungry for food
craving a hug

As the last line of elders
in the last location evaporates
Sergih's smile grows

Now,
now for the
unusual beneficiaries

Smiles cross the faces of food fighters
whose hugs extended to all
whose hands offered food
to elders living in rubble

Sergih moves deliberately with Yuliya
towards a truck tasked with transporting food
throughout Izium

They climb inside and disappear
in the dark where sun can no longer
follow

Returning with bags …
enormous bags …
of dog food

Bags hidden deep inside a truck
where food for dogs
could live with food for humans

Sergih leads us down a gutted street
off limits to cars

Foot hits broken pavement
bag on shoulder purrs
calling orphaned dogs
to come

Sergih veers from what was once a street
to what was once a sidewalk
to a place where trees and light poles
still stand

A light pole devoid of light
wrapped in PVC pipe
with a scoop at its end
kissing the ground, calling to be filled

PVC fastened to the light pole
blazing Ukrainian yellow and blue
serving as a beacon on the light pole
unable to shine

Sergih moves bag
from shoulder to ground
ringing out on contact
as dogs come and surround

Some move quickly
others are unable to keep pace
as wounds only war can inflict
limit their ability to bound
as they once did

Dogs with matted fur
dogs with gnarled knots
fur seemingly and misleadingly brushed
the furless

Homeless dogs finding their way
to a broken light pole
remembering when they were cared for
by family

Dogs whose families
have fled, have sadly died
whose homes are now in ruins

Small barks find voice
not directed at other dogs
but gently encouraging
Sergih and Yuliya

Bag of food opens
hands reach in
hands still serving, connected to arms
ready to hug yet again

Hands and arms emerge with abundance
preparing to share, again

Dogs wag passionately
sensing they have been
remembered

Dogs with experience of this offering
step forward first

Step forward as missile and gunfire sound off
failing to muzzle this moment

Fearful dogs
sense safety
when nothing is safe

Face of dog disappears in Yuliya's hand
emerges chewing, looking at others
showing the way

Yuliya's joy can't be contained
and bursts through the silence
first

Deep calming laughter
does not scare dogs away
but rather calls them forth
to hands full of food
still giving

Aware the generosity
expanding in laughter
to the sound of chewing
is clearly for them

Alex
gloves off, hands full
approaches a smaller dog
who is unsure how to proceed

Trembling dog sniffs the air
takes a step filled with limp

Back leg not working
as it perhaps once did
but hovers above the ground
foot out of sync with a wagging tail

Alex steadies, smiles
finds her eyes

In captured gaze he offers food
in hand with more to give

Alex gently adjusts, gracefully moves
from a squat to a sit on the ground
edging closer, hands offering food
unthreateningly

Some bits of food fall gently
on the hardened ground
as dog looks from hand to ground
and finally approaches

His eyes lingering for one more moment
on Alex's smile
then shifts his gaze to those loving hands
trusting the offering will nourish

I am unwound
in this moment
by Alex freeing
his other hand of food

Liberated hand now pets dog
gently back and forth
across back of dog who now chews
accepting the meal, embracing the love

Dogs surround hands with food
wagging in unison
drowning out gunfire
caressed amid laughter
as joy cannot be contained

Yes, oh yes
Heaven is unfurling in joy

The Divine constantly pours out love
and care without edge or boundary or limit

And this Divine outpouring of love
is now mirrored by colleagues whose love
also knew no limits on this day
in Izium

Infectious laughter fills the air
as tails sync with the cosmos
creating a subtle hymn
married to laughter gushing forth

Gushing uncontrollably from food fighters
with heavenly backup

Laughter and love
flow as sun moves to sleep
as Heaven sings backup
and shouts for encore after encore

The laughter does not stop
joy does not wane
bags of dog food never expire

Like fish and bread for the multitudes
there was enough, more than enough [21]

Amidst the joy
Sergih fills PVC pipe

Food in hand
coupled with food in PVC
honoring today
and bridging the gap from today
to a future visit

Food shared
in and through the hands
of food fighters who saw orphan dogs
and knew their weary hands
could offer even more

Because this is how love flows
when mirroring Divine love

Limitless love to share with elders
with dogs, cats
in seamless heavenly brilliance

---

[21] Matthew 14: 13–21, Mark 6: 31–44, Luke 9:10–17 and John 6:1–14; and then
again in Matthew 15:32–39 and Mark 8:1–9

These encounters became part of the rhythm
of our work across the Ukrainian front line

A rhythm that heals
as overflowing unconditional love
is prone to do

Unconditional love
putting us all into an infectious
cosmic flow of love

To the sound of laughter
and tails wagging
in cosmic harmony [22]

[22] This amazing work continues all across Ukraine—check them out here: https://hachikofoundation.org

In Mourning and Loss

One of those times when the news
stops you in your tracks

Because steps cannot be taken
not at this moment
in July 2023

An *Unbreakable Point*
destroyed

Unbreakable Points
places of refuge dotting the front line
from Kharkiv through Kherson
and all the places in between and beyond

Housed deep underground
where bombs and evil are meant
to be kept at bay

Yet unimaginable news
reaches my ears from Orikhiv
and my feet cannot move
glued they are to street

Beyond my strength
to step away
or step forward

Because this *Unbreakable Point*
just obliterated in Orikhiv
I know particularly well

Orikhiv
a once-gorgeous city in Zaporizhzhia Oblast
endures constant shelling
and has largely been reduced
to rubble

And in the rubble
between blown-out buildings
lives an *Unbreakable Point*
where Orikhiv residents
who would not leave
could find a moment to escape

To get a haircut
in this *Unbreakable Point*

Remembering
as hair falls to floor
and barber speaks and snips
when this was normal

To take a shower
a warm soothing shower
with soap, shampoo
in this *Unbreakable Point*

Letting warm water
wash over, baptize
as lather settles for a moment
and then runs away with joy

Standing in a moment of pause
in a shower

to just enjoy, breathe, remember
when this was normal

To wash clothes
because clothes need to be washed

To sit and watch television shows
allowing a moment of escape
because escape is needed

Maybe a comedy to provoke laughter
because laughter cannot be forgotten

Or a love story imploring hearts to swell
because hearts need to swell

To be offered a cup of coffee, tea
with a biscuit, deep underground

A biscuit begging to be dipped
because biscuits need to swim carelessly

A biscuit softened, glorified
in coffee, tea
remembering when this was normal

A place to get medical care
as stress and trauma wreak havoc
on body, on soul

To be cared for by a doctor
who has cared for you
remembering when visiting a doctor was normal

A place holding hundreds of neighbors
blanketed in its deepest room underground
by a 20-foot Ukrainian flag kissing the wall

Names signed respectfully on the blue and yellow
of Ukraine's flag

Famous names blend seamlessly
with the names of residents who are less known
to those who do not call Orikhiv home

All residing in what was considered a safe place
in a city under siege
offering distance
underground, away from the madness

Until today
until a Russian missile descended with evil intent
as all missiles do

Until a Russian missile breached the protections
the layers of barricades and cement
breached an underground place coated in love
reducing this *Unbreakable Place* to rubble

Full of people
taking showers, washing clothes, drinking tea
basking in what they thought
was a moment of peace

I could not take another step
when the news reached my ears
and stood motionless

wet eyes closed as tears collect
as faces flash

Olya ...

Peace
peace be upon her

A baker with a knack for fancy cakes
decorated to invite wonder and awe

Whose creations took us
beyond our ability to hold
with only our eyes

A baker who decided to stay in Orikhiv
despite the constant bombardment

Even though she and her husband
had passage and means to escape

A baker who would not
leave her neighbors

A baker who made an oven
with her own hands
spilling over with love

An oven made underground
in defiance of the shelling
so bread could be baked
even though her city was cut off

Cut off from major towns
in the vicinity

cut off from other parts
of Ukraine

Seemingly cut off
from the world

Who woke every day to bake
because bread must be broken and shared
in community

A baker who could not leave Orikhiv
for her daughter's wedding
when passage was not possible
with all the shelling
keeping her from her daughter's wedding

Her daughter's wedding on the first day of July
a few days before the *Unbreakable Point*
was destroyed

Olya
peace be upon you Olya
peace …

Vitaliy …

Peace
peace be upon him

Husband to Olya
who also missed
his daughter's wedding
caring for neighbors when his daughter was wed

Vitaliy, who like his wife
used loving hands
to design and build the kitchen

So borscht and carrots and cake
could be shared with the bread
baked by Olya

So bread baked by Olya
cooked in the kitchen made by Vitaliy
could be broken, savored

Vitaliy always looked
to expand the capacity of the kitchen
so more people who needed respite
could be welcomed

Who woke every day
to let people know
they are seen, embraced

Embraced as soup moved
from bowl
to spoon
to mouth
to belly

Vitaliy …
peace be upon you Vitaliy
peace …

Iryna …

Peace
peace be upon her

Lovingly known
as Aunt Ira

A pediatrician who cared for the children of Orikhiv
making sure children grew
tending to their needs

Whose loving hands allowed children
to flourish

Who moved away from Orikhiv
when she retired

Forty kilometers away
to a quiet rural community
where she could drink tea, sit on her porch
celebrate her grandchildren

Who came back
when the war broke out
a pediatrician who returned

She never flinched as she made her way
into the shelling

Back into her community
into the *Unbreakable Point*
where people could wash and eat
and now see a doctor

Because her Divine gifts
of care and healing
would be so needed

Who woke
every day
to heal

A doctor who served meals
tended wounds
calmed souls

Iryna …
Aunt Ira …
peace be upon you Iryna
peace be upon you Aunt Ira
peace …

And Tatyana …

Peace
peace be upon her

Tatyana, who cooked the meals
people relished
in rooms
people adored

Who brought flowers
when flowers could be found
to shed a bit of warmth
deep underground
where flowers do not bloom

Tatyana cleaned every inch of kitchen
every inch of dining hall

A kitchen, a dining hall
shining bright, filled with flowers
because neighbors deserve the best

Who honored each neighbor with food
cooked with loving hands
on tables
cleaned with loving hands
across floors
mopped by loving hands
because neighbors deserve nothing less

Who woke every day
to be sure neighbors
could bring spoon to mouth
with food she prepared
with the bread Olya baked
in the kitchen built by Vitaliy
with wounds dressed by Aunt Ira

Made sure all neighbors would be nourished
in a place of dignity

Tatyana …
peace be upon you Tatyana
peace …

And as my heart swelled
to allow the volume of tears
that needed to fall find passage

I held my friends, my guides
in the beats of my heart

Held those who ran
towards the crisis

I held my friends in the Divine pause
the thin place in each heartbeat
as I stood and cried, unable to walk

I hoped Heaven welcomed them
as evil descended

Hoped God embraced them
in the moment when it all
collapsed

Hoped Olya and Vitaliy
were together, holding hands
as evil violated

Hoped Aunt Ira
had her hand on child, healing
as evil intruded

Hoped Tatyana
was serving a meal on her spotless tables
as evil unfurled

Guides holding hands
healing
serving
as they did every day

I hoped, prayed
let tears fall
in honor

Finally taking a wobbly step
in a sorrow unable
to be soothed

Thanksgiving in Kyiv

Kyiv, on a day Americans
call Thanksgiving

A day in Ukraine's capital
flooded in tears
ringing in shock

The pernicious smell
of petrol, fire, brokenness
expands as sirens wail

Floating uneasily in the smoldering wreckage
of an apartment complex
in Ukraine's capital

A courtyard littered with shattered concrete
from walls, apartment patios
that once refreshed

A street littered with unsalvageable cars
that once drove

Swing sets that once propelled children
skywards and back

Wreckage fused with strips of clothes
that once warmed

Interlaced with glass that once shielded families
from the elements

Trees blackened
limbless and still smoking

yet seemingly standing in defiance

First responders blanket the area
searching apartments
setting up medical tents
blocking streets

First responders who are tired
as such searches
are now commonplace

First responders who know
tears will flow
all day

Tears trailing the aftermath
of a missile fired into a residential complex
launched from another land

Hot soup and coffee
from deep inside a van
settle at a table
joining warm meat

A table that smells of welcome
amidst the sorrow
and the stench
calling out to counter the horror
with love

Families start to emerge
from apartments now frighteningly exposed
to the world

They are shaken
walking with unsteady legs
looking nervously at the sky
wondering why

Tentative steps and fearful glances
pause as first responders pull a body
from the wreckage

Rubble falls as body is removed
a body of a woman
covered in the white chalk of cement

Shredded clothes cling to her
holding tight, in honor
refusing to part ways

Rescuers move with sadness
with reverence
walking slowly
gurney cradling her body
her body without breath

A neighbor who was known to some
elicits shudders, sobs
as more friends will be found

People who are shaken and shaking
with trauma-filled eyes
huddle around the table

Averting eyes from path the gurney takes
as food calls and smells fight for dominance

A woman
red cap
a grey winter jacket, clearly not hers
gloveless, lips bluing
stands at the side of the table

Exposed hands do not search for pockets
shake ever so slightly

Cold wind clearly swirls between skin and fabric
as jacket simply does not fit

A hot cup of coffee
is offered

Coffee cup is clasped
with both hands, without looking
as table calls out and smells try
to call her back

Hands encircle the cup
whose warmth does not stop
the tremors

Time passes
tremors continue
no coffee passes her lips

Cup loses its warmth
and is replaced by another

Time keeps passing
and this woman
in red cap and ill-fitted winter coat

suddenly, unexpectedly returns

Ever so slightly
returns to herself

She places cup of coffee
on the table
begins to gather food

Soups pile up
on a corner of table
she humbly makes
her own

Buckwheat and sausage fill one container
then another, another
placed gently next to soup

Sandwiches and coffee follow
until her corner of table
overflows in food, smell, warmth, abundance
standing in all the unfolding sorrow

She pauses and considers
how best to carry
this outpouring of love
in the form of food
back home

She looks up
eyes stray from center
shakes of hands now engulf her entire body
as she teeters on becoming lost
yet again

Her corner of the table
built with such care
is simply too much for her to carry
in gloveless hands and ill-fitting winter coat

This is noticed, leading to hands of food fighters
reaching out, gathering food
amassed on the corner
calling out for support

A thin place flickers
just beyond eyesight
just beyond heartbeat

Opening as burdens are lightened [23]
as warmth is amassed and carried
for a woman with still-shaking hands

A woman
who frailly came back

Thin place accompanies woman and food fighters
as food is moved from corner of table
into arms

Thin place journeys as neighbors are passed
with food in hands on an unsteady pathway
towards an apartment complex
not directly hit but severely damaged

Dark entrance greets
as electricity has vanished
and will perhaps return, one day

---

[23] Galatians 6:2

Stairs shrouded in darkness allow passage
as food is carried and thin place accompanies
a woman
home

Upward to a hallway
that takes over for the stairs
with a door barely discernable
in the dark

Thin place continues its journey
as food and people enter an apartment
barely illuminated by a dim light
burning further down a hall

Debris crackles underfoot
as food moves towards light

A table shakes in hallway
barely touching the light
reaching out for more

Dust covers table
a vase lies on its side, barely holding on
some flowers still cling to vase
while other flowers lie untethered from vase
once quenching water scattered rootless on floor

A picture on table looks out sadly
the woman in red cap is beaming
in the embrace of a man and surrounded by children
from a time before horror struck

A family captured in embrace
from a before time

Debris noise reverberates under foot
communicating approach with every step

Light illuminates a living room
where family huddles on broken chairs
sits on floor
in front of a gaping hole

A hole once full of
wall, windows, patio
which once allowed its family to manage
their engagement with the outside world

The light is natural
streaming through gaping hole
telegraphing a simple message—nothing now separates them
from the November cold

The man from the picture
on the shaking table, in the hall
stands in gaping hole

Trying to tape a plastic sheet from ceiling to floor
where patio once settled

Trying to keep cold
at bay
perhaps trying to keep future bombs
away

Searching for solitude, privacy
from the madness

Plastic sheet
like the jacket the woman wore
is ill-fitting

Sheet will never cover the gap
never stop the cold, never withstand another bomb
never offer the solitude
this family so desperately needs

Photos from a time before memories
could be stored, reclaimed from a cloud
litter the floor

Photos of family through the ages
some in color, many in black and white

Living now in mangled frames
covered in dust now consuming the room
when gaping hole was created

Ancestors clinging to small pieces
of damaged glass
watching and praying

Walls littered with busted hooks
where pictures once lived comfortably
once positioned in a prime vantage point
to watch this generation's lives unfold

An old clock lies motionless on floor
confirming time has stopped

Heaven is inexplicably present
amidst the carnage
the terror, shock, loss

Heaven present in room
where ancestors look on with sadness
time halts unmercifully
not a word is spoken as no words
can be found

Where not a tear falls
as tears have already fallen

In a room where a man was failing
to cover an ultimately uncoverable hole

Heaven is present, accompanying in sorrow
as a gentle warmth pushes back the cold

An unmistakable warmth felt by all
not needing confirmation

The woman, cap removed, jacket discarded
lips returning from blue
now holds her child in the protective way
mothers know instinctively

She no longer
shakes

Food carried by food fighters
is laid out with care
on what remains of a table

A wounded table in a living room
welcomes food in remembrance

of meals shared at table
in the not-so-distant past

Meals shared
in thanksgiving
in love

An elderly woman
who welcomes like a grandmother
sighs and straightens
brings soup to lips
followed by meat
chewed slowly
as Heaven warms

She shares a piece of remaining meat
with child in mother's embrace

Child accepts offering
closes eyes
nestles more securely
into warmth offered by mother
magnified by Heaven's warmth

Unspoken honor is extended
to the man trying so hard to rebuild

Not an ounce of scrutiny
fills the air

The air is instead filled
with the warm tenderness
of a child being tucked in

Ancestors look on from the floor
with steadfast determination to witness

Broken glass
dirt and dust
bits of frame
fail to block
ancestors' sight

Ancestors insisting on their presence
as Heaven wraps all in embrace

A comforting stillness descends
as the earth spins a little less violently
as breath synchronizes with Heaven

And a father looks at his family
with eyes that comfort
nodding to all
as child chews
with eyes closed
in embrace of mother

A Thin Place Recipe

A hand reaches with Divine intent
for a pot
as chefs do across Ukraine
every day in this war

Pot drawn from a rack
or a closet
from atop a table
or from the back of a car
from what was once a house

A pot calling for food
blessing food

A pot in the hands of a chef
who will marry ingredients
in unity, illuminating a thin place
inviting entrance

A flame is lit
from a stove, a gas burner
or born of wood

A lit flame to warm a pot
where food will gather to nourish
illuminating a thin place on a cold winter's day
in Ukraine

Olive oil lubricates the warming pot
awaiting additional ingredients to join
when time is right

No sleeping at this moment
as Yeshua warned
be ready when the time is ripe [24]

The call from pot is heard
as chef moves with grace
to respond to yearning
from warmed pot ready to feed

Beets glow
carrots startle
garlic sizzles
potatoes embed
cabbage fills
tender meat moistens

Ingredients enter, dance, blend, soften
knowing their purpose
will illuminate a thin place
inviting entrance

Gallons of broth join the ceremony
allow ingredients in warm pot
to swim

Individual ingredients
in communal harmony
awash in Divine *shem* [25]

---

[24] Matthew 25:1–10

[25] Aramaic for atmosphere or sound vibrating, calling, linking to breath as
beautifully revealed in Neil Douglas-Klotz, *Revelations of the Aramaic Jesus:
The Hidden Teachings on Life & Death* (Charlottesville VA: Hampton Roads
Publishing, 2022), 17.

Stirred by gentle hands
with taste buds stimulated and aglow
stirring, as chefs are known to do

Spirit glows in witness
participating through the loving hands of chefs
orchestrating this glorious meal
with eyes full of heart

Stirring and waiting and tasting
knowing when it is ripe
in this thin place, inviting entrance

Salt enters last
to make this meal complete
to create perfect harmony
elevating the offering into cosmic perfection
never losing its savor [26]

Thin place basks
as pot sweetens

Ingredients maintaining their unique gifts
while simultaneously
blessing and enhancing others' unique gifts
to create a borscht
to witness, to nourish

Ingredients dance
on a thin place dance floor
in a pot on a flame
stirred with loving hands
and eyes full of heart

---

[26] Matthew 5:13

Borscht moves from flame to truck
nestled by other foods on journey
to those who await

Driver with Divine intent
traverses battered roads, checkpoints, danger
bringing gift of love infused
with the Divine intent of chefs
to the front line

Guests from bunkers, rubble, damaged homes
come as food moves from truck to table

All are welcome
all invited as the table expands
to include all [27]

A bowl held by shaking hand
from cold, fear
comes forth from a guest
whose own loving hands
and own eyes full of heart
cannot be contained any longer

Spirit pulsing unconstrained
as ladle dips ever so gently
into pot aglow to meet bowl in hand

Words of gratitude, of recognition
exchanged over borscht singing
of thin place, inviting entrance

---

[27] Matthew 22:9–10

Heartbeat slows
as borscht descends

Stomach fills
as borscht coats

Legs and feet find balance
as borscht transforms

Smiles return
as smiles are missed

These moments of connection
build Heaven on earth

As chefs connect with drivers
blessed by those who keep food supplies moving
uniting in service

Seasoned with subtle whispers of love
embracing people on the front line
to share moments of peace
in a war that makes no sense

Bowls filled every day
stomachs nourished every day
hearts open every day
as Spirit celebrates
to the brim and beyond

Closer to the Light

I have heard people fall asleep
counting sheep
one, two, three

But I can't count sheep
as we have no sheep
anymore

I count explosions instead
one, two, three

But I can't sleep
when counting explosions

Words she would share later
when safe, underground

Because right now it is not safe
above ground

Her words would resonate
as explosions are met
by a woman who opened a door
beckoning us to enter

Drones scanning
missiles descending
on a snowy grey day in Huliaipole

Opened door leads to underbelly
of deeply wounded apartment complex
with no tenants above ground

Stairs shake with each step
creaking out warnings
groaning under the strain of war

Stairs give way to faintly lit hallway
calling us from darkness
closer to the light

We enter a makeshift kitchen
flame bursting from wood scraps
warming a pot
smelling of another time

Bag with logo from those who care
lies empty next to stove

Kitchen blends into a makeshift room
where a faint light searches from a lightbulb
dangling from ceiling
trying to shed more light
but too weak to illuminate all

A table, some chairs
seven beds huddled together in makeshift room
smelling of another time in condolence

Natalia welcomes us in
asks our names and leaves to stir food
in pot on flame

She returns with a gift
fried pieces of dough
made from contents

of bag with logo
sprinkled with sugar, sprinkled with love

Warm on lips
sweet on lips
comforting as drones circle above

Light tries to stretch and meet us all
as Natalia speaks of how blessed she is
to live underground

I used to live in an apartment
where I could see the sky
an apartment now gone

Along with my beloved husband
who Russia stole

I was lost in sorrow when the missile came
and stole my husband
stole my apartment

All my friends have left
and I became a stranger in this city
I call home

No home to lay my head
no husband to make me laugh
no friends to comfort me

Where could I stay?
where is my home now?

Until I was called inside to this room
so drones and missiles
would not so easily find me

I now sleep in this little room
where 6 women
6 strangers made room for me

As she speaks
the light who has tried so hard
to spread glory glows a bit stronger
as Heaven smiles

I am the chef
of this little kitchen

I care for the strangers
who welcomed me in
who gave me a home

Light spreads as we all find ourselves
closer to the light
illuminating Heaven's smile

The dough
still sweet, warm
tastes even grander
as the beauty of Natalia's words penetrate

Yeshua loved strangers
honored them in parables
to illuminate God's Realm
on earth [28]

Yeshua was famously grateful
to be fed, offered drink, welcomed
when it was easier to be refused [29]

---

[28] Luke 10:25–37
[29] Matthew 25:35

Yeshua implores us to replicate
acts of welcome
gestures of compassion for and to all [30]

Light glows brighter
Heaven smiles wider
as Natalia asks if she could prepare
a meal for us when we come back
next time

Spoon moves through pot on flame
eyes looking down, heart wondering
how we will respond

We sing *yes*

Natalia is asked what we can bring
to share as part of this blessed feast

A feast cooked by a chef
who was a stranger and is now a friend
who was without home and has now found home
underground

Bathed now in glorious light bursting from a lightbulb
bubbling with heavenly joy
contained in a smile blanketing the cosmos

This question startles
as Natalia stirs
unsure

---

[30] Matthew 25:40

I do not know
we have been given food
but never asked such a question

Into the ensuing silence
is suggested ... a cake

Perhaps a cake

Natalia visibly stumbles backward
as light catches her and heavenly smile expands

Hand places spoon to stir on table
hand reaching instead for forehead

A tear builds, falls

I am a baker living underground
cooking in a glorious kitchen
where I sadly cannot bake

I have forgotten what a cake
tastes like

Tears explode from eyes
as light expands and holds

Yes, I would so love
so love to remember
what cake tastes like

Sobs fill the room
illuminated by heavenly light
bursting from bulb
as Natalia starts to speak again

In the stuttering voice
one emits
when words are stirred with sobs
as Heaven smiles
and light extends

Could you …

Could … you …
also bring …

Could you also

Bring …

Some sparkling … water

Sparkling water to wash down

Wash down

The cake … whose taste …
I have … forgotten

Drones no longer circle
missiles fall silent
as we stand bathed in light

Strangers creating Heaven
in a makeshift kitchen
underground
closer to the light

The Miracle of Peace

Miracles happen
even in war

A family who rushes to the front line
to feed and comfort
when others might rightly choose
to run away

Sergih nourishes Ukrainians
across the highly contested oblast
known as Donetsk

Katerina feeds and cares
for the well-being of food fighters
across the country who experience trauma
as well

Daughter Sophia
wise, courageous beyond her 14 years
feeds and nourishes and cares
with mom, with dad

They focus on the elderly
on children
on dogs and cats
and have amplified their offerings

Blending food and hot soups
with clothes and boots
as clothes in Donetsk are tired
boots worn thin

New offerings of hygienic products
some designed for all
some designed specifically for women
now move with food to care for the people
of Donetsk

New offerings accompany food
like crayons and paper
because children need to imagine

This family
Sergih
Katerina
Sophia
see beyond food

They see beyond food
because they pause and listen
even as explosions try to halt dialogue

Pause and listen so that words
expressing need amidst the sounds
of sirens and weaponry
can be honored

New offerings blend seamlessly into their mission
to support all who remain
delivered into those impossible places
in their beloved Donetsk

When words like *impossible* descend
as such words often do
they can translate into *inaction*

The *inaction* meaning someone
will not be helped

This family and their team
deliver into *impossible*
making their offerings tangible

Tangible to the families
who remain heads down and trembling
as Russia
obliterates Bakhmut

To the families who live in the middle
between armies outside Kostiantynivka

They wake every day, dreaming of peace
making sure Ukrainians who shake from cold
from military thunder
from uncertainty
are seen, embraced in their beloved Donetsk

They dream of peace
and imagined a larger family
in that time before war

A brother or a sister for Sophia
another daughter, another son
for them

But for over a decade before the time of war
they remained three

Sergih and Katerina and Sophia
remained three while dreaming of more

Oh yes miracles do happen
when we least expect it

Mary knows [31]
Zechariah and Elizabeth know [32]
Sara knows [33]

Sergih and Katerina
beyond all expectations
conceived and birthed
a daughter in a war

With a name offered
by a 14-year-old daughter
blessed by a family
a family that fed and cared for so many
in their beloved Donetsk

Solomiya

A name of Hebrew and Ukrainian
creativity and imagination

A name filled with hope blesses
a name meaning
peace

Solomiya was placed lovingly in my arms
by mother who offers peace to all

---

[31] Luke 1:26–38
[32] Luke 1:5–22
[33] Genesis 18:10

This miracle stretches
nestles and settles against my chest
holding my finger as babies are known to do

And I am swept away
swept away by peace
as breath syncs
as sleep descends
as Heaven opens
opens in peace

The room is noisy, but we are quiet
as adult heartbeat and breath
moves in rhythm with heartbeat and breath
of peace

Without prompt, without thought
my heart pounds a question
a question heard by peace

A question from before times
gushing from Yeshua
who is blooming right now
unfolding in the noise yet quiet
in synchronized heartbeats and breath

Unfolding and reminding
that we must become like little children
to truly see [34]

Tell me
please tell me
what it was like

---

[34] Matthew 18:2–4; Mark 10:15

Being in the presence of the Divine
feeling the Divine's radiance
before you came
before peace came
came to bless all
in this unspeakable war

Solomiya hears the question
in her heart, answering from beyond

Her finger unmistakenly tightens its grip
embracing my finger with a strength and comfort
that defies expectation

With a grip holds
not letting go
as babies are known to do

Embracing as the Divine
is known to do

Peace sighs while finger is gripped
sighs in that tone from before time places
as babies are known to whisper

Speaking in a soft whisper
to comfort and strengthen
as the Divine is known to do

Peace opens eyes and glances
with eyes carrying deep wisdom
soothing as babies are known to do

Gazing beyond
as the Divine is known to do

Gifts infused with Divine offering
conveyed by a miracle baby
in a war transmitted from peace
emanating from Solomiya

Reminding us to embrace
hear, see beyond
gifts the Divine planted in us all

Peace tumbles forth
and Solomiya invites a wider gaze

As heartbeat and breath
lead me into an ancient knowing wisdom
Yeshua suggested illuminates all

To a place to honor those
like her parents, like her sister
who run towards the fire
towards those left behind

Harnessing bodhisattva energy [35]
bringing tikkun olam to life [36]
walking paths of generosity and service
as Yeshua and others model

Drawing Divine cosmic vitality
unwilling to pause
until Heaven is built
until peace truly descends
right here on earth

---

[35] A being on the way to enlightenment who turns, and returns so that all can be relieved of their suffering

[36] The Jewish passion to meaningfully heal, to concretely repair, our broken world

I hold Solomiya as Heaven unfolds
surrounded by parents, by sister
by Yuliya and Josh and Alex and Olha

People who I have witnessed
run towards the fire to feed and nourish
those who so easily could be left behind

And I see beyond those who sit with us
as heart and breath remain locked in harmony
with unfolding Heaven

A cosmic harmony extended to those
all over this planet who wake every day
to say no to the madness

Shard seekers
first responders
search and rescue crews
neighbors whose doors are always open

Food fighters and cooks
who create moments of Divine grace
when borscht flows from pot to bowl to lips to belly
and nudge us home

Storytellers and activists
who use film, words, art, presence
to capture Divine love unfolding
even in horror

And all those whose sacrifice
is rarely seen, rarely celebrated

Essential "behind the scenes" people
who secure funding
give generously
manage finance and logistics
so people on the front line
can be seen, can be fed

To those who extend hands and heart
to the modern-day lepers
modern-day deaf
modern-day marginalized
whom we so often push away
whom we claim don't quite sync

Who see the unhoused as Yeshua modelled
who stand with orphans and widows as Yeshua modelled
who do not demonize people seeking refuge
as Yeshua modelled

When all this is seen with a broader lens
seen with these eyes of peace and wonder
we see the Divine
unfolding before us

We discover with this broader gaze
a different army
one that perhaps seems outmatched

An army that wakes every day
to build Heaven on earth
in simple and grand, selfless gestures

An army resisting the madness
seeing Divine sparks everywhere

whose actions irrigate the cosmos

Some walking in Yeshua's *shem*
his aura
his atmosphere
to serve and witness

And those whose paths are set to the music
of other healers and visionaries
charting new paths of wonder
illuminating Heaven on earth

Spreading love and care
ignoring modern-day Pharisees
who limit, exclude, and falsely qualify
conditions for Divine unfolding here on earth

An army that wakes every day
to build Heaven on earth
from the rubble we all make

This magnificent Heaven
on this wondrous earth
in this astounding cosmos

Solomiya   .

Afterword, In Loving Honor of Damian Soból

It's still cold as spring teases
in Colorado

I walk, surrounded by mountains
with dog on one side
walking stick tapping its song
on the other

Walking stick blesses and mourns
blesses and mourns
with each tap
in rhythm with breath
in rhythm with step

A series of bombs in another war
have taken
have taken friends

Friends who fed
fed and witnessed
fed and comforted
fed with eyes full of heart
fed those who have nowhere
nowhere to go

Fed people in this particular chapter
of this particular bloodbath
in a place called Gaza
that long ago lurched into the absurd

My walking stick
sings in mourning
sings as it blesses
lost lives

A few lost lives I knew well
drowning in a sea
of lost lives in an absurd war

The rhythm of the walking stick
carries me back to Ukraine
reuniting with
a brother

A brother whose glow from unselfishness and care
embodied a thin place
he gave away, effortlessly

Heaven on earth, wrapped in a thin place
visible in smile
felt in warmth
spread in laughter
infectious in silliness

Expressed to the world
with his characteristic
open arms in embrace of all

Embracing and living a love
that must overflow
even in war

Walking stick sings as I recall
how he met me upon arrival in Krakow

and how he brought me to Ukraine
every time

Walks me across the border
from Poland to Ukraine
hugging me and smiling

Keep your head down because we need
to get you back home

And with that he left
as we pulled into Ukraine

I always turned as we pulled away
to marvel as he extended open arms
to us and beyond us, embracing the world

When I return to the border
on the Ukraine side this time
he awaits

With a smile, extending open arms
in welcome to us and beyond us
embracing the world

Let's get you home
home to your family

We walked again
from Ukraine into Poland
getting back to Krakow so I could return home

And when we parted ways
he would always turn
extending open arms

to me and beyond me
embracing the world

These walks across borders
were technically unnecessary
as I have been crossing borders
all my life

But they were offered in boundless generosity
living what Yeshua taught us

To walk further and beyond
what is asked

When someone wants your tunic
give your cloak as well

When someone slaps your right cheek
offer left cheek as well

Do not turn away but give
give when asked
give when evil confronts [37]

Ensuring Divine companionship flourishes
so that I could get home
from the front line

Now this brother
like so many siblings who rush towards chaos
changed lives

Changed lives and lived in embrace
in relationship

---

[37] Matthew 5:38–42

though these siblings
are so rarely seen, so rarely sung

But on this day as spring teases in Colorado
walking stick will not be subdued
but sings

Sings of a brother who found car parts
when car parts could not be found
so food could reach
reach the front line

Walking stick sings
sings of a brother
who found food
when food could not be found
so food could reach
reach the front line

Walking stick sings
sings of a brother
who guarded assets
and set up kitchens
and warehouses

When assets and kitchens and warehouses
were needed
so food could reach
reach the front line

And walking stick sings
sings of a brother
who walked those extra steps
with extended arms open

embracing the world

Colorado is cold on this day
as tears flee from eyes
and walking stick inhales
in silence

Arms extend as he taught
embracing the world
as he taught

With words pouring forth
words not my own
borrowed words for this moment

> All those things in the world to which this day will bring increase;
> all those things that will diminish; all those too that will die;
> all of them, Lord,
> I try to gather into my arms,
> so as to hold out to you in offering.

—PIERRE TEILHARD DE CHARDIN, *Mass On The World* [38]

---

[38] De Chardin, Pierre Teilhard *The Heart Of Matter* (San Diego, William Collins Sons & Co Ltd., 1978), 120.

Acknowledgments

When you have grown still on purpose while everything around
you is asking for your chaos.

—MIRABAI STARR [39]

Heaven bursts. Heaven pulses. Everywhere. All the time. All around
us. Inviting entrance and offering us all a chance to embrace Heaven,
on earth, as imagined in that time before time.

Yet I need guides to help me see and experience Heaven unfolding all
around.

This book is a love letter to those guides, whose courage, generosity,
selflessness, and care opened my eyes to the glory vibrating all around
us. Even in a war.

It is impossible—simply impossible—to understand the wonder of
this humanitarian effort and the love that flowed through food, hugs,
and compassion without centering Yuliya Stefanyuk. She is the rock
on which all this work is built, and her ideas, her vision, her ability to
listen to others and incorporate their wisdom into the delivery of food,
seed, water, lights, and care to Ukrainians across the front line allowed
so many people who have been forgotten in the horror of this war to
be seen and fed. I see Heaven bursting with every step she takes.

A core team of the bravest people I know must be celebrated. Their
ability to support each other, to constantly ensure that beautiful
food passed from lips to belly, and their relentless search for
people who could easily be forgotten allowed Heaven to manifest

39 St. Teresa of Avila, *The Interior Castle* (New York, Riverhead Books, 2004),
Introduction by Mirabai Starr, 3.

as bombs dropped. Their compassion makes Heaven unmissable. Ukrainians across the front line are blessed to have this core team of humanitarians waking every day to remember them, to honor them, to witness their pain, and to comfort when comfort is needed as much as food.

Join me in honoring the Onishchenko family—Sergih, Katerina, Sophia, and Solomiya—as well as Alex Denisenko, Olha Maksiuk, Kateryna Lymarenko, Evgeny Lymarenko, Inna Kushnir, Ruslan Vyhovskyi, Yuliia Vysytska, Anton Baranov, Julia Konovalova, Chef Polina Sycheva, Iryna Lychak, Denis Kondaurov, and Kyrylo Kolisnyk.

We had a local finance team whose care was felt in the field and whose enhanced scrutiny enabled more people to be fed. Thanks to this team who included Iryna Lytvynchuk, Kseniia Zvantseva, and Elena Olenichenko.

A local monitoring team was focused on identifying those most in need, working on strategic ways to withdraw from communities as other actors entered with food, and who made sure food got into Ukrainian bellies as planned. They included Olga Zaitsev, Anton Baranov, Yuri Shaynuk, Vladimir Berezhnyi, Olena Tsimbalyuk, and Ruslan Vyhovskyi, and were supported in profoundly empowering ways by Josh Balser.

And we had hundreds of people who worked in warehouses and drivers who navigated unpredictable situations on bombed-out roads—all of whom made sure Ukrainians were fed. No food and care would have happened without them!

Heaven was revealed through food, cooked by chefs and in restaurants all over the country, who were supported by the brilliance of chefs from outside of Ukraine who came, encouraged, and shared. This web of Ukrainian chefs seasoned with chefs from around the world helped Ukrainians living in fear settle and find their feet when inside they were falling. Restaurants across Ukraine responded with grace and courage in the face of evil, and I am blessed to have witnessed compassion and care bubbling from the kitchens run by chefs and restaurateurs like Oleksii Shpionov, Zhanna Nikonova, Laert Arutiunian, Dmitro Vysotskyi, Elena Vasylenko, Ruslan Ovcharenko, and Roman and Katya Denisov. The team of Misha, Kolya, and Costin ran our food truck in Mykolaiv, which, along with Chef Oleksii, inspired the chapter "A Thin Place Recipe."

We worked with over 120 restaurants across the front line—some in backyards after their formal restaurant was shelled. This community continues to startle and inspire, and I thank them all and hold all in my heart. Both the people named above and the unnamed who together saved lives.

I found that I could settle enough to experience Heaven because of a security team whose dedication to this work was astounding. People who woke every day to make sure we were all safe, so that people could be fed and comforted across the front line, creating the space for Heaven to blossom as food flowed regardless of the dangers posed. I am forever grateful to this team that was led by Szymon Kowal and included but was not limited to Pan Maciek (Shorty), Mariusz Jandulski (MJ), Grzegorz Gural, and Andrzej Szum. Our team was supported with such grace and impact by Arek Kamecki and brother Damian Soból from Poland.

A global team provided support, encouragement, and witness to the team in Ukraine. I was flooded with compliments directed at this team of leaders, who travelled to the front line in support of Ukrainian food fighters and who made them feel less alone. People who made our Ukrainian colleagues more seen.

I am most grateful to Josh Balser and Courtney Koos whose leadership and support was transformative. Chefs Elyssa Kaplan, Olivier de Belleroche (Chef Oli), and Ric Miller who inspired; a US-based finance team who helped make sure food could reach the front line, especially Anya Graziano Shova, Rhea Ilagan, and Val Gonzalez; a fundraising team who kept Ukraine front and center and inspired so many to help our Ukrainian colleagues with their generosity, including but not limited to Maggie Leahy and Daniel Poole. A procurement team who found whatever was needed to get food to the front line— Matt Tognarelli, Kristin Irani, and Matt Magnuson. A data team that made sense of it all including Adina Elena Anton, Brian Chan, and Brian Stoll.

Storytellers shape the world, and we were blessed to walk with storytellers who honored the team and who made sure Ukraine was never forgotten. They included Aleksandr Golub, Mykola Kulina, Sebastian Lindstrom, Lisa Abrego, and Samantha Higgins.

I am forever grateful to Erich Broksas, whose friendship and professional partnership for close to two decades flourished even more fully when we were together at World Central Kitchen. My heartfelt thanks to Erich and the Executive team for blessing me with the opportunity to witness such wonder.

I was especially fortunate for the support I received from Fatima Castillo who was lead on this program before I joined and whose care in implementing during the early days of the war and in transitioning this work to those of us who followed was seamless and nourishing. I am deeply grateful to Felix Carver who assumed the lead role upon my departure and wakes every day to make sure people are fed and staff are safe.

This work across the Ukrainian front line was launched, shepherded, and cared for with courage and compassion by Nate Mook. Nate has rightly received considerable recognition and honors from President Volodymyr Zelenskyy for his ongoing commitment to Ukraine, including but not limited to his role in the Hachiko Foundation celebrated in the chapter "Dogs Come Running."

This manuscript has been greatly enhanced by a community of friends who have walked with me in the most important ways for significant parts of my life. They offered support, encouragement and editorial finesse all along the way. Deepest thanks to Paul Robinson, Elisa Speranza, Pat Sormani, Gregg Burch, Aaron Doverspike, Aram and Ellen Haroutunian, Andrea Wait, Tom Scanlon, Sarah Borgman, Wende Valentine, and Dawne Taylor, and my spiritual director Sister Mary Colleen Schwarz, OBS and her fellow sisters at Benet Hill Monastery whose prayers and love carried us all.

A special thanks to an immensely talented group of writers who read every word, helped me change direction when a change of direction was desperately needed, and whose wisdom and words enrich these pages. They collectively made this experience of writing so much more bountiful—Elyssa Kaplan, Patty Koscinski, Peter Nagle, Morgan Grace Milburn, Patrick Reis, Doug Norfleet, and Ryan Hansan.

Blessings to the team at Wild Rising Press, Judyth Hill and Mary Meade, for their faith in this project and their care in the story's telling—who taught as well as brought this work to completion and cannot be thanked enough.

And finally, to my beloved spouse Lindsey and my daughters Kimberley and Jemma, whose love, courage, support and compassion embrace and carry me every day.

Author's Biography

In the wake of the Russian invasion of Ukraine in February of 2022, Ned Breslin ran one of the largest humanitarian operations across the vast, decimated Ukrainian frontline. Prior to his work on the ground in Ukraine, Breslin and his team ensured water was reestablished to kitchens and communities following natural disasters across the globe as World Central Kitchen's Water, Sanitation and Hygiene Director.

Best known for his transformative work in global water and sanitation, Breslin pioneered a radically different approach to district- and city-wide programming that ensured that every family, school and clinic in participating cities and districts had access to sustainable water and sanitation. This work, with the global NGO Water For People and others, ignited a global sector reboot that will support over 200 million people by 2030.

Breslin is a recipient of the prestigious Skoll Award for Social Entrepreneurship because of his leadership in international water and sanitation and has been leading humanitarian relief and development programs throughout the world since the early 1990s, including a 16-year period when he and his family lived in southern Africa.

Breslin is a graduate of the Living School, a unique program in Christian mysticism based at the Center for Action and Contemplation, founded by Father Richard Rohr. It is through this transformative experience that he became attuned to the constant availability—even in war—of Divine presence.

Breslin lives with his spouse in Evergreen, Colorado, and can be found hiking its seemingly endless trails and fishing its majestic rivers, while continuing to serve in humanitarian operations around the world.

The body text of Ned Breslin's *Praisesong: Delivering Food on the Ukrainian Frontline* is set in Adobe's Devanagari — a typeface whose development represents two thousand years of deep cultural and linguistic history. Devanagari, an ancient Indian script developed from Brāhmī script, was used for over 120 languages, including Hindi, Marathi, Nepali, and Sanskrit. Using this one script to unify the scripts of Indian dialects was itself revolutionary. The Adobe Devanagari Font Family, designed by Fiona Ross, Robert Slimbach, and Tim Holloway for Adobe Originals, profoundly respects the script's historical roots and the practical needs of contemporary design. Both elegant and culturally sensitive, an Adobe Originals' global font initiative, Devanagari means "heavenly script of the city of the Gods or priests," and is the quintessential pairing for Breslin's heart-lifting, heartbreaking tales of sacred service to an ancient and brave people. Devanagari's balanced proportions and thoughtful spacing mirror the lyrical resonance of these passionate, long-form narrative poems.

The titles herein are set in Bell MT italics developed in 1788 by the punchcutter Richard Austin for the British Letter Foundry, later digitalized by Monotype. An elegant serif font with refined curves, Bell Italic reflects the excellence in font design made possible by advances in fine book printing in London at the time. Its slight slant lends a sense of forward motion that presages the hopefulness felt in each section. This typeface shares with Devanagari a common homage to ancient linguistic and literary tradition. The opportunity to publish this exquisite volume is an enormous privilege; through editorial, proofreading, and design at every stage, our Press never lost sight of the tremendous importance and honor of offering these poems and sharing, with the author, this act of sacred witness.

www.ingramcontent.com/pod-product-compliance
Lightning Source LLC
Chambersburg PA
CBHW071006120626
46546CB00003B/952